A Kid's Guide to Drawing America™

How to Draw
Florida's
Sights and Symbols

Jennifer Quasha

The Rosen Publishing Group's
PowerKids Press™
New York

To Mica and Isabella

Published in 2002 by The Rosen Publishing Group, Inc.
29 East 21st Street, New York, NY 10010

First Edition

Book and Layout Design: Kim Sonsky
Project Editor: Jannell Khu

Illustration Credits: Laura Murawski
Photo Credits: p. 7 © Museum of the City of New York/CORBIS; p. 8 (photo) by Juan Brown; p. 9 (painting) Painting Compliments of the A.E. Backus Gallery; p. 12, 14 © One Mile Up, Incorporated; p. 16 © Bill Ross/CORBIS; p. 18 © Lynda Richardson/CORBIS; p. 20 © David Muench/CORBIS; p. 22 © Richard Cummins/CORBIS; p. 24 © James L. Amos/CORBIS; p. 26 © Joseph Sohm; Visions of America/CORBIS; p. 28 © Tony Arruza/CORBIS.

Quasha, Jennifer.
How to draw Florida's sights and symbols / Jennifer Quasha.
p. cm. — (A kid's guide to drawing America)
Includes index.
Summary: This book explains how to draw some of Florida's sights and symbols, including the state seal, the official flower, and the Magic Kingdom's castle.
  ISBN 0-8239-6064-1
1. Emblems, State—Florida—Juvenile literature 2. Florida in art—Juvenile literature 3. Drawing—Technique—Juvenile literature [1. Emblems, State—Florida 2. Florida 3. Drawing—Technique] I. Title II. Series
  2001
  743'.8'09759—dc21

Manufactured in the United States of America

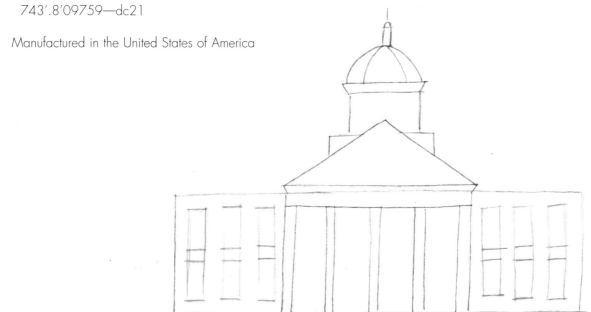

CONTENTS

Let's Draw Florida

Along with oranges and Walt Disney World, the state of Florida is known for its abundance of water. Florida is surrounded by nearly 8,500 miles (13,679 km) of coastline and has many lakes, rivers, springs, marshes, and creeks. Florida's big industries include banking, electronic equipment, insurance, and tourism. In fact, more than 40 million people from all over the world visit Florida every year for its beautiful beaches and to enjoy the famous SeaWorld and Walt Disney World resorts.

Florida has a rich history. Florida used to be home to about 200,000 Native Americans called the Seminoles. The word Seminole is from the Spanish word *cimarrones,* which means "free people." These proud Native Americans were given this name because they resisted being made slaves by the Europeans. Florida's city of Saint Augustine boasts the oldest permanent European settlement in the country. People have lived in Saint Augustine since 1565!

With this book, you can learn more about Florida's history and some of its key sights and symbols. You can begin drawing the sights and symbols from simple shapes. The step-by-step instructions and red guidelines in this book will show you what to do from there. The last step of most of the drawings is to add shading. You can add shading by tilting your pencil to the side and holding it with your index finger. Before you start, make sure you have all the supplies on hand and a clean, well-lit space where you can draw comfortably.

The supplies you need to draw Florida's sights and symbols are:

- A sketch pad
- An eraser
- A number 2 pencil
- A pencil sharpener

These are some of the shapes and drawing terms you need to know to draw Florida's sights and symbols:

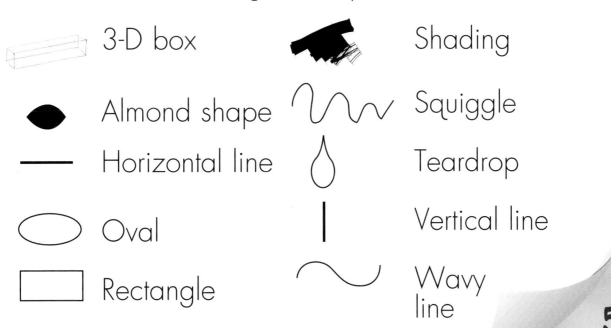

3-D box

Almond shape

Horizontal line

Oval

Rectangle

Shading

Squiggle

Teardrop

Vertical line

Wavy line

Land of Flowers

The first Spanish explorers, including Juan Ponce de Leon, reached Florida's shores in 1513. Ponce de Leon claimed it for Spain and named it *La Florida*, which means "land of flowers." Around this time, Europeans believed that Florida was full of gold. In the late 1580s, English explorers like Sir Francis Drake came to Florida in search of wealth. Britain gained control over Florida in 1763, at the end of the French and Indian War. Although ownership changed hands a few more times, future U.S. president Andrew Jackson established a new American territory government in Florida in 1821. On March 3, 1845, Florida officially became the 27th state to join the United States.

Today, Florida is populated by more than 14 million people. It has the oldest population in the United States. More than one in five people living in Florida are over age 65. Florida's capital city is Tallahassee, which has a population of about 136,000 people.

Andrew Jackson was the seventh president of the United States. He held office from 1829 to 1837.

Florida Artist

Photo by Juan Brown

Albert Ernest Backus

Albert Ernest Backus was born on January 3, 1906, in Fort Pierce, Florida. He took summer classes at the Parsons School of Design in New York City, but much of his artistic training was self-taught. He read about different artists and their styles of painting and then experimented on his own.

Backus loved children and spent much of his time with kids in his art studio. Kids who visited his studio earned the nickname Backus Brats. He opened his studio to these kids to encourage them to develop their creative talents.

One of Backus's own major influences was the work of Claude Monet, the French impressionist painter. In much of his early work, from the 1930s to the 1950s, Backus used colors similar to the colors in Monet's paintings. In these earlier works, Backus used a palette knife instead of a paintbrush to get the same effect as Monet. Although he was influenced by the French painter's techniques, Backus's subject matter was closer to home. Backus focused on Florida's landscape and was one of the few artists to paint Florida's natural beauty in the twentieth century.

In Backus's later work, he used a paintbrush to re-create Florida's landscapes. He liked to paint in the early morning or late afternoon because of the interesting ways the light affected his subjects during those times of the day. Backus often was seen sketching in Fort Pierce even in the years just before his death in 1990.

Painting compliments of the A.E. Backus Gallery

Backus painted Indian River Sunrise in 1980. It was done in oil on canvas and is 16″ x 20″ (41 cm x 51 cm). This painting captures Florida's rugged landscape and the state's beautiful morning light.

Map of Florida

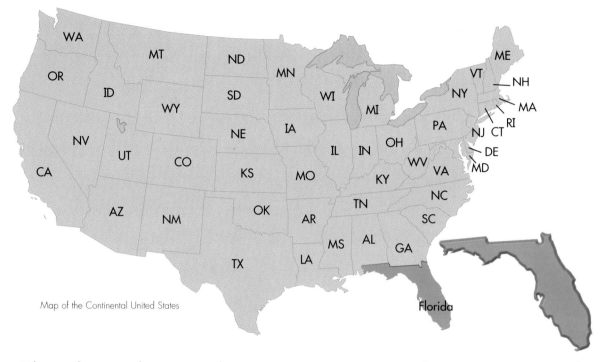

Map of the Continental United States

Florida

Florida is the southernmost state in the continental United States. It is a peninsula that borders the Atlantic Ocean and the Gulf of Mexico. The state's major cities include Tallahassee, Miami, Jacksonville, Saint Petersburg, and Orlando. Florida borders Alabama and Georgia. Florida has two national forests, Ocala and Apalachicola National Forests, and Everglades National Park. Florida's Big Cypress National Preserve borders Everglades National Park. Lake Okeechobee, one of Florida's largest lakes, spills into the Florida Everglades 100 miles (161 km) away. A 150-mile-long (241-km-long) chain of islands off the coast of Miami makes up the Florida Keys.

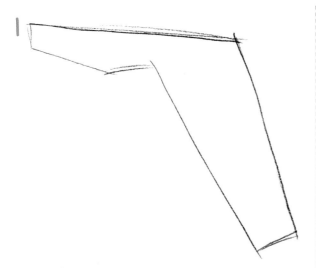

I

Draw the angled shape as shown.

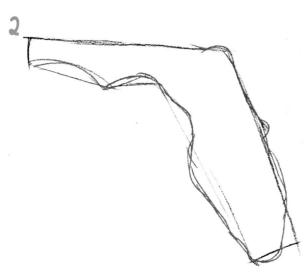

2

Add curves to the angled shape.

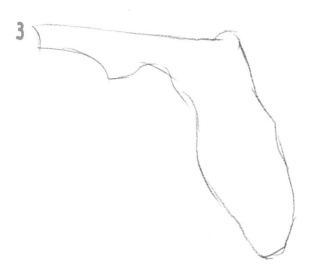

3

Erase the extra lines. You just drew the outline of the state of Florida.

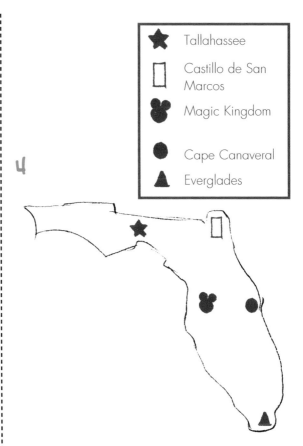

4

★ Tallahassee
▯ Castillo de San Marcos
❀ Magic Kingdom
● Cape Canaveral
▲ Everglades

a. For Tallahassee, the state capital, draw a five-pointed star toward the upper left area of the state.
b. Draw a vertical rectangle in the upper right. This is the location of Castillo de San Marcos, in Saint Augustine.
c. Draw a circle on the right side of the state. This is the location of Cape Canaveral.
d. For the Magic Kingdom in Orlando, draw a circle. Now draw two smaller circles on top of it. You just drew Mickey Mouse's head!
e. At the bottom of the state, draw a triangle as shown. This is the location of the Everglades.

The State Seal

Florida's state seal was adopted on August 6, 1868. In 1970, the state legislature recommended some changes be made to the seal. The changes were made in 1985. The tree in the seal was changed from a cocoa tree to a sabal palmetto palm, which became Florida's state tree in 1953. The words around the border of the seal read "Great Seal of the State of Florida" and "In God We Trust," the state's motto. The most important image on the seal is of a Native American Seminole woman scattering flowers on the ground. Beyond the woman, sun rays beam out above the sea and land. In the background, a steamboat travels on the water.

1

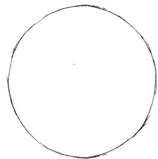

Draw a circle as shown. For neat circles, draw around a mug or a jar lid.

2

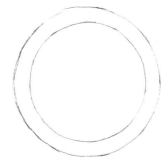

Draw a smaller circle within the first circle.

3

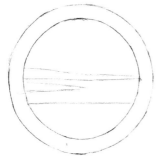

Lightly draw horizontal lines across the seal. This is the land.

4

Lightly draw the palm tree in the center of the seal as shown. Draw an oval on the bottom right. This is a bush.

5

For the Native American Seminole woman, draw a long oval shape on the left area of the seal.

6

Lightly draw triangle shapes on the upper right area of the seal. This is the ship.

7

Great job! You just laid out all the main sections of the seal. Now let's go back and add detail. Draw the leaves of the palm tree and bushes.

8

Add details to the woman by drawing her head, arms, and feet. Draw circles for the blossoms that are in her arms and falling to the ground.

13

The State Flag

The Florida state flag was approved in 1899. It is white with a red *X* that crosses the flag. Florida's state seal is in the center of the flag. Prominent in the seal is the Seminole woman. Seminoles were Native Americans who lived in Florida long before European settlers came to America. Seminoles call themselves the Unconquered People because they bravely fought and evaded capture by the U.S. Army in the nineteenth century. The Seminole woman on the state flag and seal helps celebrate Florida's Native American heritage and the more than 2,000 Seminoles who keep that heritage alive today on reservations throughout Florida.

1

Begin by drawing a rectangle. This is the basic shape of the flag. Use a ruler to make neat, straight lines.

2

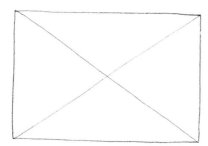

Lightly draw an *X* through the rectangle. This will guide you in the next two steps.

3

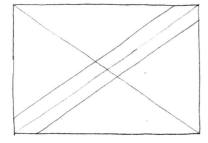

Go to the upper right corner and draw two parallel lines down to the left.

4

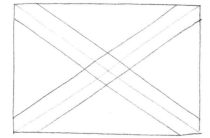

Now go to the upper left corner and draw two parallel lines down to the right.

5

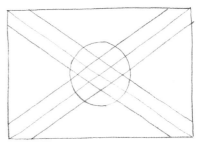

Draw a circle in the center as shown.

6

Erase the lines in the circle. Draw a smaller circle within the first circle.

7

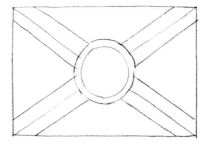

Sketch the basic features of the state seal. Draw the Native American woman, the palm tree, the ship, and the bush as shown. You can go to the state seal chapter for help.

8

Color or shade in the *X*. You just drew Florida's state flag!

The Orange Blossom

Although the orange blossom *(Citrus sinensis)* is not native to Florida, it was chosen as the state flower in 1909. Explorers most likely brought orange trees to Europe from Asia. From there, Europeans brought them to America.

Orange blossoms grow on orange trees all over Florida. They are small, white flowers with a beautiful and fragrant smell. Orange trees provide Florida with one of its most well known products, oranges, and also the state beverage, orange juice! In addition to nicknames like the Sunshine State, the Alligator State and the Everglades State, Florida often is called the Orange State.

1

To begin, draw a circle. This is the bud.

2

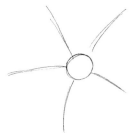

Draw five curved lines that fan out from the bud. These lines will help you draw the petals.

3

Use the curved lines as guides to draw the petals as shown.

4

Continue drawing the petals.

5

Toward the right side of the bud, draw a small circle. Draw another smaller circle within that circle.

6

Great job! Now draw more buds to the lower left of the flower. Draw three ovals and connect them to the flower with curved lines.

7

Behind the flower, draw four curved leaves that come to points. Lightly draw the lines inside the leaves. These are the leaves' veins.

8

Shade in the area around the bud and the tips of the petals. You just drew Florida's orange blossom!

The Mockingbird

The mockingbird became Florida's state bird in 1927. The mockingbird is known for its beautiful song and its ability to copy the songs of other birds. There are ten different species of mockingbirds, but they all look similar. Males and females are the same size and are about 10 inches (25 cm) tall. In flight, their wings reach about 15 inches (38 cm) across. Mockingbirds are mostly gray with white underbellies and white markings on their tails and wings. The male and female live together in a bush, in a nest made of grasses and twigs. Females lay three to six pale bluish green eggs with brown spots.

1

Draw an oval at an angle. This is the body of the bird.

2

Draw a circle on top of the oval. This is the head.

3

Draw lines that connect the head to the body. Extend the lines to draw the beak and tail as shown.

4

Great job! To draw the wing, make an upside-down teardrop shape on the body as shown.

5

Draw the legs and feet as shown.

6

Complete the feet. Add the claws by making little hooks. Draw the eye and extend the line from the beak under the eye as shown.

7

Draw the feathers on the wings as shown. You just drew a mockingbird!

19

The Sabal Palmetto Palm

In 1953, the sabal palmetto palm was chosen as Florida's state tree. This tree grows all over the state because it can grow in many different types of soil. The sabal palmetto palm's trunk is tall and thin and has no branches. Its grayish brown bark looks smooth, but is rough to the touch. The sabal palmetto palm's green leaves are thick and leathery and can be as large as 4–7 feet (1–2 m) long. The leaves are wide and fan shaped. This palm bears black fruit that measures ⅜–½ inch (1–1.3 cm) wide and grows in clusters up to 7 feet (2 m) long. The sabal palmetto palm is also known as the cabbage palmetto, tree palmetto, and Bank's palmetto.

1

Draw a tall, thin triangle shape at an angle.
This is the trunk.

2

Turn your pencil on its side and lightly
shade the upper part of the palm tree. This
is the palm area.

3

Draw the palms by making hook shapes on
top of the shaded area. Don't worry about
making perfect palms. Just have fun drawing!

4

Add details to the palm leaves by drawing
lines that extend downward as shown.

5

Shade the areas between the palms. Draw in
the lines on the trunk. Great job!

The Zebra Longwing Butterfly

The zebra longwing butterfly became the state butterfly in 1996. The butterfly is mostly black with yellow stripes. These butterflies are commonly seen in Florida's Everglades National Park, which covers 1.4 million acres (566,560 ha) of the state's southern tip and is the largest subtropical wilderness in the nation's 48 contiguous states. During the day, the zebra longwings fly slowly in a zigzag fashion. Their favorite food is the nectar of passion flowers. The zebra longwing stays with its family in a group that rests together in the same area each night. These butterflies sleep so soundly that if you pick up one butterfly from the middle of its group, none of its family members will wake up!

1

Draw the shape as shown. This is the butterfly's left wing.

2

Draw the same shape, but flipped, next to the first one. This is the butterfly's right wing.

3

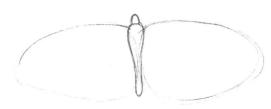

For the butterfly's body, draw the shape between the wings as shown. For the head, draw a small oval shape on top of the body.

4

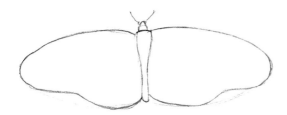

Draw antennae on top of the head. Draw a line across the middle of the head. Add detail to the bottom of the wings as shown.

5

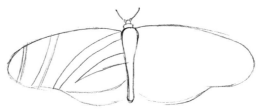

Add eyes to the head. Now draw the stripe design on the left wing of the butterfly.

6

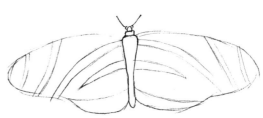

Carefully draw the zebra stripes on the right wing exactly as you did on the left wing.

7

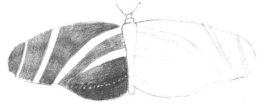

Begin shading the left wing as shown. Be patient and shade slowly.

8

Now shade the right wing and the body of the butterfly. Good job!

23

Castillo de San Marcos

The Castillo de San Marcos is located in Saint Augustine, Florida. Construction began in 1672 and ended in 1695. The fort was built by Spanish colonists for protection against pirates. The fort was built with coquina, a limestone rock made from seashells and coral. When the United States purchased Florida in 1821, the fort was renamed Fort Marion. Afterward it was used as a military prison and a storage facility. The fort, an example of seventeenth-century military architecture, was once entirely surrounded by a moat. Some of the unique places to see in Castillo de San Marcos include guardrooms, watchtowers, and the gun deck.

Draw the square at an angle as shown. This is the center of the fort.

2

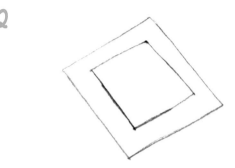

Draw another square outside the first square.

3

Connect the outer square with lines as shown. Nice job. You just drew a 3-D box!

4

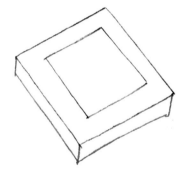

Connect the lines in the center of the squares as shown. Now you've added depth to the 3-D box.

5

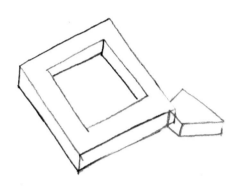

Draw the 3-D triangle shape on the bottom right corner as shown.

6

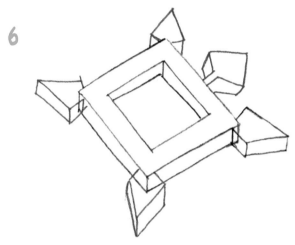

Before you start, carefully study the red guide shapes. Now draw the 3-D triangle shapes on each of the corners. Draw an additional triangle shape in the center right. Notice how the shapes are all different on each corner.

7

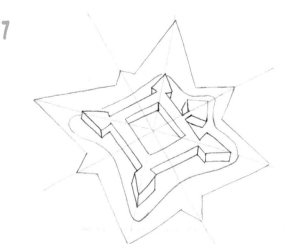

Lightly draw four lines that intersect the monument. Use them as a guide to draw around the fort, then erase them.

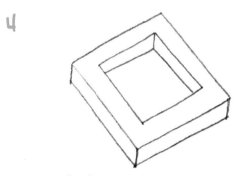

Florida's Capitol

Florida has an old capitol building and a newer capitol building. Both are in Tallahassee. In 1824, three log cabins served as the state's capitol building. The government grew, and a brick building was built in 1845. In 1902, a dome was added and two wings were built to make more space. By 1911, the state's government was too large to fit in one building. Officials had to work out of many different buildings. Finally, in 1972, money was granted to build a new capitol complex, which was completed in 1977.

Today government officials work in the new capitol building, while the old capitol building serves as the Department of State's Museum of Florida History.

1

Begin by drawing a long rectangle. This is the base of the capitol. A ruler will help you draw clean lines.

2

Divide the rectangle into three sections. The middle section should be slightly larger.

3

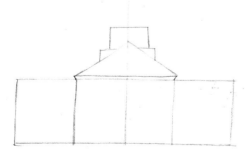

Slightly above the middle section, draw a triangle as shown. Now connect the triangle to the rectangle by drawing little angled lines.

4

Draw a rectangle behind the triangle as shown. Erase any lines that cut across the triangle. Draw another rectangle on top of the first one. This is the base of the dome.

5

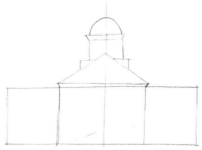

Slightly above the rectangle, draw a semi-circle for the dome. Draw a horizontal line underneath the dome. Now connect the dome to the rectangle with the angled lines.

6

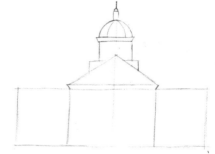

Add lines in the dome as shown. Draw the minidome on top of the first dome.

7

Draw vertical lines in the rectangle. These are the columns.

8

Draw more vertical and horizontal lines in the outer rectangles as shown. These are the windows of Florida's capitol building.

27

Walt Disney World Resort

Walt Disney World Resort covers 43 square miles (111 sq km). It is the world's largest entertainment compound. Walt Disney World is in Orlando, Florida. More than 200,000 people visit every day, and its hotels accommodate more than 50,000 people each night. It boasts amazing theme parks, including Epcot Center, the Magic Kingdom, Disney-MGM Studios, and Disney's Animal Kingdom. The resort has more than just theme parks. Restaurants, golf courses, shops, rides, and shows provide entertainment all day long and make it one of the top travel destinations for families in the United States.

1

Draw the basic castle shape of the Magic Kingdom. Notice the two sharp points.

2

Start on the left side and draw the details of the castle as shown. Notice that the shapes on top are triangles.

3

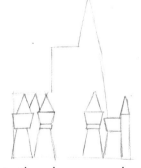

Now draw similar shapes on the right side as shown.

4

Draw a semicircle for the entrance. Above it, draw the pointed window and the details.

5

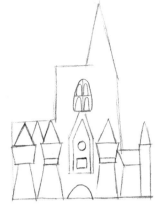

Draw more windows above the big triangle-shaped window you just drew.

6

Add more details of the castle.

7

Erase any extra lines. Draw the flags on top of the triangles as shown. Excellent!

Florida State Facts

Statehood	March 3, 1845, 27th state
Area	58,560 square miles (151,670 sq km)
Population	14,916,000
Capital	Tallahassee, population, 136,000
Most Populated City	Jacksonville, population, 679,800
Industries	Health services, communications, banking, electronics, tourism
Agriculture	Citrus, vegetables, field crops, nursery stock, cattle, dairy products
Animal	Panther
Band	Saint Johns River City Band
Butterfly	Zebra longwing butterfly
Wildflower	Coreopsis
Fish	Sailfish
Song	"Swanee River"
Soil	Myakka fine sand
Gemstone	Moonstone
Saltwater Mammal	Porpoise
Marine Mammal	Manatee
Shell	Horse conch shell
Reptile	American alligator
Rock	Coral
Beverage	Orange juice

Glossary

abundance (uh-BUN-dents) More than enough; plentiful.

accommodate (uh-KAH-muh-dayt) To make room for.

contiguous (kuhn-TIH-gyoo-us) Having contact with.

coquina (ko-KEE-nuh) A limestone rock made out of seashells and coral.

crustaceans (kruhs-TAY-shunz) Small creatures that live in the sea.

destinations (des-tih-NAY-shunz) Places to which a person is going.

fragrant (FRAY-grint) Something that smells.

French and Indian War (FRENCH AND IN-dee-un WOR) The battles fought between 1754 and 1763 by American colonists, England, France, and Native Americans for control of North America.

keys (KEEZ) Small, low islands.

moat (MOHT) A deep, wide ditch that surrounds a castle or a town for protection against an enemy.

palette (PA-lit) A thin, oval board that artists use to mix their paints.

peninsula (peh-NIN-suh-luh) A piece of land that sticks out into water from a larger body of land.

prominent (PRAH-mih-nent) Very easy to see because it stands out in some way.

Seminole (SEH-mih-nohl) A tribe of Native American Indians who lived in Florida.

species (SPEE-sheez) A single kind of plant or animal.

subtropical (sub-TRAH-pih-kuhl) An area that borders a tropical area.

zigzag (ZIHG-zahg) A line, pattern, or course that moves in or has a series of short turns from one side to the other.

Index

Web Sites

To learn more about Florida, check out this Web site:
www.state.fl.us